Pasta! Pasta! Pasta!

A collection of pasta recipes
compiled and edited by Ursel Norman
Designed and Illustrated by Derek Norman

**William Morrow
& Company, Inc.**
New York

Published in Great Britain
under the title *Pasta & Oodles of Noodles*.

Printed in Great Britain.

Library of Congress Catalog Card Number 75-0510
ISBN 0–688–02922–1

Contents

Introduction

Pasta. From where did it come?

The origin of pasta has long since been lost in the mists of antiquity. The myth that pasta was introduced into Italy by Marco Polo does indeed seem mostly myth. For there appears to be a noticeable absence of any evidence to suggest that it might be historical fact. More credible is the theory that pasta was eaten by the Romans some considerable time before Marco Polo's travels to China.

Certainly the evolution of pasta has been typically Italian. Where else could such a basic staple as pasta have found expression in so many different forms and variations? Many have magnificently sculptured shapes, like miniature works of art, all touched by the Italian genius for recognizing no separation between art and life.

Such a complex heritage may explain why there are so many misconceptions surrounding the cooking and serving of pasta, all doing a gross injustice to the gastronomic feats and delights of Italian pasta cookery. Many people believe that pasta amounts to nothing much more than spaghetti, macaroni, ravioli and something they serve in the local Italian restaurant, called lasagne. Alas, what masquerades as a pasta dish in many so-called Italian restaurants is at the very best a pale imitation of the real thing.

It is sad that pasta cooking with its multifarious tastes and nutritional values has been too often carelessly practised. For pasta is a subtle, immensely versatile food, that is also satisfying, inexpensive, easy to prepare and, contrary to popular belief, low in calories. Low in calories in-so-far as a little pasta goes a long way, leaving the stomach feeling full and contented for hours.

For the Italians, pasta is not so much a meal as a way of life, such is their passion for pasta with its many colorful and regional variations. The joys of pasta can be as complex or as simple as you like – many Italians treasure as simple a dish of pasta as spaghetti tossed in olive oil with a grating of black pepper.

Should you wish to venture deep into the gourmet delights of pasta, try making your own dough from scratch. Homemade pasta may sound like a near impossibility – rest assured, it is not. It can be mastered very quickly for it requires no special skills – only patience and a little practice. Once mastered, the results can be most gratifying. Exquisite homemade ravioli with a filling of juicy, delicately flavored meat or aromatic cheeses. Or cannelloni, stuffed with a succulent beef-and-spinach filling. Or tortellini with a characteristically Italian filling of ricotta cheese.

There are also the delights of regional sauces with their pungent flavors of herbs and spices, such as Genoese pesto, with its flavoring of fresh basil (it is worth giving up a little corner of your garden to grow it) and the ever-famous and versatile bolognese sauce.

In this book you will find a collection of traditional recipes with the flavor and sumptuous delight of Italian cooking. In selecting the recipes an attempt has been made to balance the many regional flavors of Italian cooking, using only the traditional ingredients – although you may find it necessary to compromise from time to time. Taking into account the availability of certain ingredients I have indicated alternatives when they might seem necessary.

The design of this book we hope reflects our love of pasta. For selecting the recipes and preparing the drawings have been an absolute delight, to which our stomachs can well testify. Our Look and Cook format has been devised for ease of use and understanding, so that at a glance the reader can comprehend how a dish is prepared and how, finally, it should look when it reaches the dinner table.

As a footnote to this introduction, we would like to express our grateful thanks and appreciation to our publishers for their kindness in allowing us to produce this book. We are also indebted to many friends who have offered suggestions in the preparation of the manuscript – in particular our old friends Carla and Frankie Mondolfo in Rome and Elizabeth Cox in London. Their assistance has been invaluable.

And lastly, we hope the reader will find this book a practical, no-nonsense kind of cookbook. One to be looked at and enjoyed, but, above all, to be used.

Buon Appetito!

Ursel Norman
Derek Norman

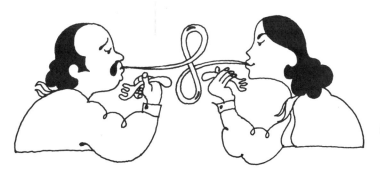

How to Please Your Pasta

(and make oodles of beautiful noodles)

A basic guide to some of the Dos and Donts of pasta cooking.

Pasta-making

Store-bought pasta, even the domestically produced kind, is usually of excellent quality. However, like most other commercially produced foods, it is never quite as good as the homemade variety. So I feel everyone should give pasta-making a try. It is not as difficult as it may sound and is a very satisfying thing to do. Of course pasta-making is a necessary task for the preparation of ravioli and tortellini; these are of doubtful quality when store-bought.

Making the dough is really easy; rolling it out requires a little practice. If you are doing it for the first time, don't make it on a busy day. Slowly does it. And remember to keep your working surface well floured at all times; pasta dough gets quite sticky when it is rolled out. Don't worry about too much flour sticking to the dough – it will all come off in the cooking water.

To make egg-noodle dough
4 large eggs
4 tablespoons cold water
about 1 pound (4 cups) all-purpose flour
1 Break the eggs into a large mixing bowl. Add the water and about a quarter of the flour. Beat this mixture with a wire whisk until it is very smooth.
2 Add nearly all the rest of the flour and work the mixture with your hands into a soft dough. If the dough seems sticky, work in the rest of the flour. (The absorbency of the flour can vary from one bag to the next, as can the size of the eggs.)
3 Turn the dough out onto a kneading surface and knead it well for 10 minutes, just as you would a bread dough. This will extract the gluten content in the flour and give the dough its elasticity.

4 Put the dough back in the bowl, cover it and leave it to rest for at least 20 minutes. (In no way can the dough be rolled out until *after* a lengthy rest period; it would just pull back on you.)
5 Roll the dough out to a thickness of $\frac{1}{8}$ inch. You may find it easier to cut the dough into two pieces first, and roll them out separately. They will be more manageable that way.

To make green-noodle dough
One 10-oz package frozen chopped spinach, cooked, or 1 pound fresh spinach, cooked and chopped finely
4 large eggs
$\frac{3}{4}$–1 pound (3–4 cups) all-purpose flour
1 Drain the cooked spinach well and squeeze as much as possible to remove the cooking water. The more expert you are at this, the less flour you will need, and your noodles will be greener.
2 Break the eggs into a mixing bowl. Add the spinach and a quarter of the flour. Beat well with a wire whisk until the mixture is smooth.
3 Add the rest of the flour gradually, then follow the instructions for egg-noodle dough from stage 2 down.

Pasta by Machine

For those cooks who become pasta addicts, it is well worth acquiring a pasta machine. The machines make an excellent job of kneading and rolling out the pasta and cutting the noodles. And it needn't be an expensive machine, either. The cheaper ones are just as efficient at rolling out the dough, but they have fewer blades and don't cut quite as many different shapes. But they all cut egg noodles and flat sheets, really the basic requirements.

Shaping of Pasta

Shaping the pasta is the fun part. There are hundreds of different pasta shapes. The basic commercial ones are passed through dies and emerge as long, solid rods. These are spaghetti of various thicknesses. The next step is to push a metal rod through the solid strand, and these emerge as macaroni. Then come all the fancy shapes of twists, curls, shells, rings, ribbons, tubes, stars, etc. The easiest and most popular ones to make at home are those cut from flat sheets of pasta, which are then called noodles. You make these as follows:

Roll the flat sheet of dough up from one side to the other, like a jelly-roll (Swiss roll), and cut slices off it with a sharp knife. Unroll the slices and lay the noodles flat on a piece of well-floured waxed or grease-proof paper. Leave them to dry for 10–15 minutes before cooking.

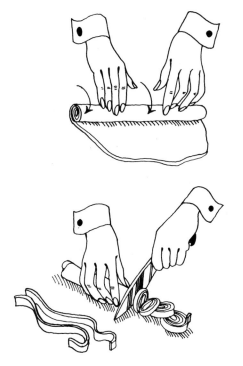

For tagliatelle: cut the roll into $\frac{1}{2}$-inch thick slices

For fettuccine: cut the roll into $\frac{1}{4}$-inch thick slices

For fettucce: cut the roll into $\frac{1}{2}$–$\frac{3}{4}$-inch thick slices

Pappardelle are cut from a flat sheet of dough into strips about $\frac{5}{8}$ inch wide. Cut them with a fluted pastry wheel rather than a knife; this will give the noodles their characteristic edges. Dry them for only 5 minutes before cooking.

Also from flat sheets are cut the following:
manicotti: cut into 3-inch squares
lasagne: cut into 4 × 10-inch rectangles
cannelloni: cut into 4-inch squares
(Don't dry any of these; cook them as soon as you can.)
Any left over pasta dough can be gathered into a ball and rolled out again, to be cut into noodles, or it can be cut into small squares for soups. These are called pastina or quadrucci.

Storing Pasta

Noodles which are not cooked straight away after the specified drying period should be left out on floured waxed paper until they are completely dry. This takes at least one day. They will then resemble commercially produced pasta and should be stored as such, in paper bags or cardboard boxes, to allow for air circulation. Dried pasta will keep for months without refrigeration.

Filled pasta such as ravioli and tortellini cannot be dried because the filling will spoil. They can, however, be frozen. Place them in rows on floured waxed paper, not touching or they will stick together. Roll them up in the waxed paper, then wrap the roll in foil and freeze.

Cooking of Pasta

Pasta needs to be cooked in a large pot, with plenty of water to float around in. It should never be crowded into a pot or it will stick together. For the same reason you should not use a metal spoon for stirring; a wooden spoon or, better still, a wooden fork does a much more efficient job.

As a rule, 1 pound of pasta requires at least 4 quarts of water and 1–1½ tablespoons of salt. But do not add the salt until the water boils, and only just before the pasta goes in, otherwise you get an odd side taste. The pot should never be more than partially covered.

Long, thin pasta should not be broken into pieces. Immerse it as far as it will go in boiling water; let it fan out at the top. Then bend in the middle and force the rest under water with a wooden fork. Other pastas should all go into the pot at the same time, otherwise some of it will be cooked more quickly than the rest, and nothing is as bad as overboiled pasta.

Store-bought pasta cooks much longer than fresh, homemade pasta. Follow the package directions, or better still, bite a piece now and then. The pasta should be soft, but with a slight resilience in the centre. This is the *al dente* stage, and the stage at which most Italians serve their pasta. However, you may like yours a little bit harder or softer than that, but bear in mind, it should never be mushy.

Homemade, fresh pasta cooks very fast:

Egg noodles, yellow	5–6 minutes approximately
Egg noodles, green	4–5 minutes approximately
Lasagne	2 minutes
Manicotti	2 minutes
Cannelloni	2 minutes
Tortellini	5–8 minutes
Ravioli	5–8 minutes

These are rough guides; the best guides are your teeth. As a general rule, homemade pasta is cooked when it rises to the top of the pot.

Pasta Serving

Most commonly pasta used to be served as a first or second course, to be followed by the main course or entrée. It is still frequently served this way in many restaurants in Italy, but at home it has become more of a main dish. This seems to be the way most people prefer their pasta.

If pasta is served as a first course, 2–3 ounces of pasta per person is plenty. It should then be served in rimmed, small bowls and eaten with a fork.

However, if pasta is served as a main course, you have to judge the amount of pasta per person by your guests' appetites. Main-meal pasta can be served on a dinner plate, and it makes a delicious, satisfying and usually inexpensive meal when served with some fresh crusty bread and a crisp tossed salad. Followed by some fresh fruit, this is one of the most nutritious meals you can serve.

Cheeses for Pasta

The most commonly used cheeses in pasta cookery are cheeses for grating. And the two most popular and easily obtainable ones are parmesan and romano, in that order. Ideally it is best to use the imported kinds, for their quality is immensely superior to the domestic variety. However, if you cannot get the imported kinds, domestic brands are adequate. Real imported parmesan should be at least three years old and golden in color. Romano cheese is white.

Neither cheese should ever be bought already grated. Once grated they soon lose their pungency and taste of very little more than plastic. No complement to a lovingly prepared dish. Do not grate the cheeses until just before you plan to use them.

Grated parmesan is passed with just about every dish of pasta, but never with fishy ones. The sharp flavor would distract too much from the delicate taste of the fish.

Ricotta cheese is used mainly for fillings of stuffed pasta and is readily available in most large supermarkets. Cottage cheese, which looks similar, is only a substitute, which should only be used if ricotta is absolutely unavailable.

Mozzarella cheese is commonly used in baked dishes, since it acquires its characteristic stringyness only when it is hot. It is a mild, somewhat creamy, cheese.

Ingredients in Pasta Cooking

Most of the different kinds of pasta used in this book are easily obtainable. Supermarkets carry a surprising variety. Grocery stores in Italian neighbourhoods are a fine source, of course. If you have trouble tracking down a particular shape, ask your grocer to get it. It is not difficult for him to find it among the many brands on the market.

The herbs in this book are also readily available in dried form. Fresh ones one never sees in the supermarkets, but they are such fun to grow in the garden or in a flowerpot.

Most people believe that the Italians use a lot more garlic than they do. Indeed, many use it only sparingly. Then there are people who consider garlic in a sautéed form too heavy to digest, and prefer to add it later, together with the sauce. See which way you like best. There is also a rule that if a dish contains tomatoes, any cooking oil may be used for the sauté stage. However, if a dish does not contain tomatoes, olive oil is essential to enhance the authentic flavors.

Any pasta used in this book may be exchanged for another shape of pasta if desired. There are no hard and fast rules as to what goes with what. Personally, I do prefer the larger pasta shapes with those succulent meat sauces, so the sauce will cling to the grooves, little bits of meat get stuck in the crevices and fill up the inside – yum!

The meat content in my recipes is usually rather higher than Italian cookbooks suggest. This is because I believe that most people will want to serve pasta as a main course. As indeed a lot of Italians do. So the nutritious value of the dishes has been taken into account. Four ounces of meat per person does not seem extravagant. Italian cookbooks usually suggest 2 ounces per person. I prefer to give up authenticity for nutritious value here.

Of course, the pasta itself, even the store-bought variety, has a high nutritious value, being made of good flour or semolina flour with wholesome additions of spinach or eggs, or both.

Note I like to pour off the accumulated fat by setting the lid askew, only leaving a tiny crack for the fat to escape through. You can pour the hot fat straight down the sink, provided the cold tap is running. The cold water will flush the globules down smoothly.

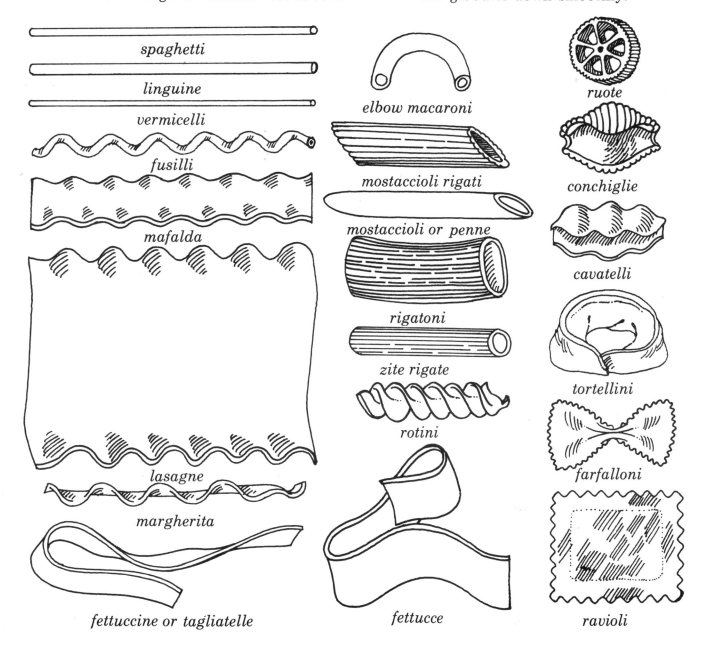

spaghetti

linguine

vermicelli

fusilli

mafalda

lasagne

margherita

fettuccine or tagliatelle

elbow macaroni

mostaccioli rigati

mostaccioli or penne

rigatoni

zite rigate

rotini

fettucce

ruote

conchiglie

cavatelli

tortellini

farfalloni

ravioli

3 tablespoons butter
4 slices bacon, chopped
1 large onion, finely chopped
1 medium carrot, finely chopped
1 stalk celery, finely chopped
2 tablespoons oil
$\frac{1}{3}$ pound ground beef
$\frac{1}{3}$ pound ground pork
$\frac{1}{3}$ pound ground veal

$\frac{1}{2}$ cup white wine
2 cups good beef stock
3 tablespoons tomato paste
1 teaspoon dried oregano
a little grated nutmeg
salt and pepper to taste
1 cup heavy cream (or to taste)
1 pound spaghetti
grated parmesan cheese

1   Melt the butter in a frying pan and in it sauté the chopped bacon, onion, carrot and celery. Cook, uncovered, stirring frequently, for about 10 minutes. Set aside till needed.

finely chopped   bacon chopped   finely chopped   finely chopped

2   Heat the oil in a heavy saucepan and in it brown the meats, breaking up any lumps with a wooden spoon, until the mixture is brown and crumbly. Pour off the accumulated fat using the saucepan lid.

nutmeg   beef   veal   pork

3   Put back on the fire and stir in the wine. Cook over high heat until most of the wine has evaporated. Stir in the beef stock, tomato paste, oregano, nutmeg, salt and pepper, and the reserved vegetables and bacon.

4   Simmer this sauce, only partially covered, until it has reduced to a thick sauce, about 40–60 minutes. Add all or some of the cream, but do not boil again!

5   Cook the spaghetti in plenty of boiling water (add salt when boiling) until *al dente*. Drain.

SPAGHETTI

6   Serve the pasta on hot plates, with some of the sauce spooned on top. Serve plenty of grated parmesan cheese with this dish.

Note   This sauce is equally good over any noodle or macaroni, or any of the larger pasta shapes, such as rigatoni or shells.

Spaghetti Bolognese

This was probably your first introduction to pasta as a child – or so you thought. A familiar name – but have you tried the authentic version? The smooth and delicate tasting bolognese sauce is distinguished by the addition of fresh cream and aromatic vegetables. Savor this simple dish and discover the real thing, Bologna style. The children will love it! (Serves 4)

4 tablespoons butter
½ cup heavy cream
6 tablespoons grated parmesan cheese
salt and pepper to taste
8 oz fettucce

3 Cook the fettucce in plenty of boiling water
(add salt when boiling) until *al dente*.
Drain well.

1 Melt the butter in a small saucepan over a low heat.
Don't let it brown.

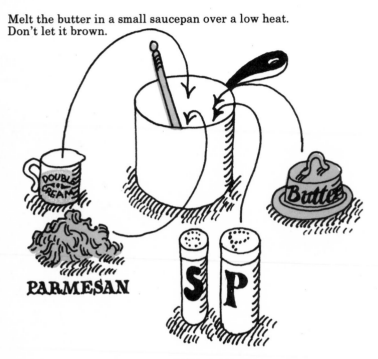

2 Off the heat add the cream and the grated parmesan.
Put back on the fire to heat the sauce through
and melt the cheese. Do not boil, however, because of
the fresh cream. Stir in the salt and pepper.

4 Combine the noodles and the sauce and leave
to stand, covered, for 2 minutes before serving.

Pass more grated parmesan cheese if you wish.

Note You can substitute fettuccine for fettucce.
Homemade noodles are especially fine for this dish.

FETTUCCE ALFREDO

This dish is named after Alfredo, owner of the famous
restaurant *Alfredo* in Rome. It makes a first course for four –
one of the pure pasta dishes that distinguish themselves by their earthy
simplicity. It has a delicate, unbelievably creamy taste
and may also be served as a main course or as a
great accompaniment to fried, grilled or roast meats.

1 recipe egg-noodle dough from page 8
1 small onion, finely chopped
2 tablespoons oil
1–2 cloves garlic, crushed
1 pound ground beef
2 tablespoons grated parmesan cheese
2 tablespoons chopped parsley
1 teaspoon salt
a little grated nutmeg
one 10-oz package frozen spinach, cooked and chopped
   or 1 pound fresh spinach, cooked and chopped
2 eggs
1 recipe salsa di pomodoro from page 64

5 With your index finger press down between the fillings to seal them in. With a fluted pastry wheel or a sharp

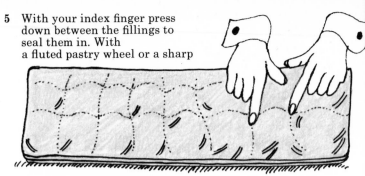

knife, cut the ravioli into 2-inch squares. Seal the edges firmly by pressing the seams together all around, either with your finger or with a fork. Set the ravioli aside on well-floured waxed paper until all ravioli have been made.

6 Cook the ravioli, a few at a time, in plenty of boiling water (add salt when boiling) until *al dente* (8–10 minutes). Drain them by removing them with a slotted spoon and proceed to boil the rest of the ravioli.

7 Spread a thin layer of the tomato sauce in a baking dish. Lay a single layer of cooked ravioli loosely in the dish. Cover with tomato sauce. Add more ravioli and cover each layer with tomato sauce to keep ravioli from sticking together. Pour leftover sauce over top of dish.

1 To prepare the filling sauté the onion in the oil until soft and transparent. Add the garlic and sauté 1 minute longer. Add the ground beef, turn up the heat slightly, and brown the beef nicely. Break up any lumps with a wooden spoon. When cooked, transfer the mixture to a mixing bowl.

2 To the meat mixture add the cheese, parsley, salt, nutmeg, spinach and eggs. Mix with a fork until well combined.

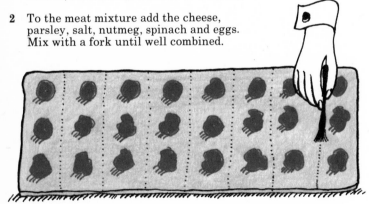

3 Divide the dough into 2 pieces, and roll each one out to a rectangle of ⅛-inch thickness.

4 Place a heaped teaspoon of filling at 2-inch intervals on one of the sheets of dough. With a pastry brush dipped in cold water, dampen a line on the space between the fillings to help seal the ravioli later. Cover the fillings with the other sheet of dough.

8 To heat the ravioli through, bake the dish, covered with foil, in oven pre-heated to (325°). This will take 15–30 minutes, depending how cold they were when going into the oven.

Note Up to stage 7, ravioli can be made 2–3 hours in advance.

16

A magnificent combination of robust tomato sauce and beef filling gives this dish a full-bodied country flavor. Home-made, old fashioned goodness.

Make them yourself and find out what real home-made Italian ravioli are like. You will surprise and delight family and friends. (Serves 4)

This is the quantity per person:

1 tablespoon olive oil
3 slices lean bacon (preferably unsmoked),
  cut into strips
1 egg, beaten
1 heaping teaspoon chopped parsley (optional)
a generous grating of black pepper
3 oz penne
2 tablespoons grated romano *or* parmesan
  cheese

1 Heat the oil in a saucepan and in it fry the bacon pieces until nicely browned. Remove the bacon with a slotted spoon and leave to drain on paper towels.

4 Boil the penne in plenty of salted water until *al dente*. Do *not* drain! With a slotted spoon remove the pasta from the water, letting it drain as much as you can. Then drop the steaming hot pasta into the egg mixture. The idea is to keep the pasta so hot that it will set the eggs slightly. Mix it all up well.

5 Sprinkle on the bacon bits and the romano cheese and toss well.

   Serve immediately, with more grated romano if wanted.

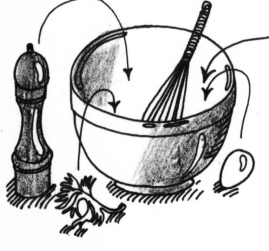

2 In a bowl combine the egg, parsley (if used) and pepper with a wire whisk until thoroughly blended.

3 Keep the egg mixture in a warm place until ready to use. (Not too hot though, or the egg would set.)

This dish is one of the most popular
in Italy, and it is fast gaining
popularity all over the world. It is one
of the quickest and cheapest of pasta
dishes, so full of goodness that it can be
enjoyed as a main course.
Truly delightful.

PENNE ALLA CARBONARA

½ recipe egg-noodle dough, cut
   into lasagne (page 9)
   or ½ pound store-bought lasagne
1 recipe ragù bolognese from page 64
1 recipe besciamella from page 64
5 tablespoons grated parmesan cheese

Bolognese Sauce

Besciamella

1 Cook the lasagne a few at a time in plenty of boiling water
   (add salt when boiling) until *al dente*. Drain them
   in a colander and leave to cool slightly.

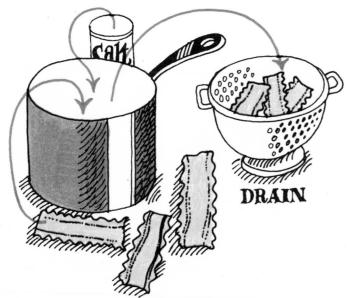

DRAIN

2 Butter generously a large baking dish or casserole
   (about 9 × 12 × 3 inches).

3 Spread a thin layer of ragù bolognese over the bottom
   of the baking dish. Over it spread ⅓ of the besciamella.
   On top of that layer ⅓ of the cooked lasagne, slightly
   overlapping. Repeat this process until all the sauces
   have been used; finish with a layer of besciamella.
   Onto the finished dish sprinkle the parmesan cheese.
   (Depending on the size of your dish, there may be
   a few noodles left over.)

3. Cooked Noodles
2. Besciamella
1. Bolognese Sauce

4 Bake the dish, uncovered, in a pre-heated oven
   (350°) for about 25 minutes if you
   are cooking it straight away, about 40 minutes
   if it has been allowed to get cold.

Parmesan

Note You can prepare stages 1–3 up to 3 hours in advance.
      Cover the dish with foil or plastic wrap until ready to bake.
      Instead of besciamella you can use cottage or ricotta cheese
      and sliced mozzarella cheese. You will need about 1 pound
      of ricotta and 6–8 oz of mozzarella.
      Layer (1) bolognese; (2) ricotta; (3) mozzarella; (4) lasagne.
      Repeat twice again, finishing with mozzarella.

Lasagne

One of the most substantial of all pasta dishes, extremely popular both in and outside of Italy. A delectable blend of pasta, besciamella and ragù bolognese makes this dish rich and appetizing. Full of nourishment, it takes a little time to prepare but is more than worth the trouble. A delightful winter meal that you will want to come back to even if it's summer. (Serves 4)

2–4 cloves garlic, cut in half
½ teaspoon dried red pepper flakes
2 tablespoons chopped parsley
5 tablespoons olive oil
1 pound thin spaghetti
freshly ground black pepper to taste

2 Cook the spaghetti in plenty of boiling water
(add salt when boiling) until *al dente*. Drain.

1 Sauté the garlic, red pepper flakes and parsley
in the olive oil for 1–2 minutes over a low heat.
Do not let the garlic brown!
Remove the garlic with a slotted spoon and discard.

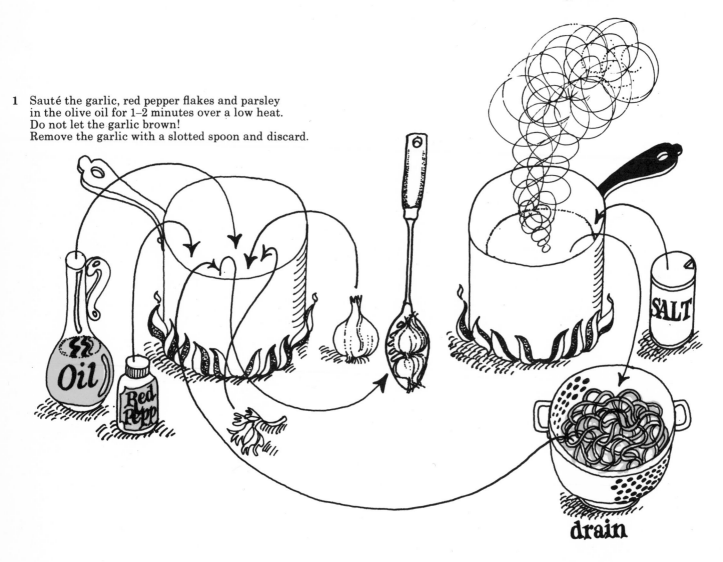

3 Off the heat, mix the hot pasta into the hot oil mixture,
season with black pepper and mix well.

Serve immediately, absolutely piping hot!

Spaghetti Aglio e Olio

One of the pure and basic pasta dishes of Italy. A simple, ingenious combination of garlic and olive oil gives this dish its smooth quality.

Quick to make, tasty and inexpensive, it is an authentic touch of Italy. Try it with a glass of Chianti. (Serves 6 as a first course)

1 medium onion, finely chopped
4 tablespoons butter
½ pound mushrooms,
  sliced and the stems chopped
salt and pepper to taste
½ pound unsmoked thinly sliced ham
  or prosciutto, cut into squares
1 cup heavy cream
2 tablespoons chopped parsley
6 oz green noodles
6 oz yellow noodles
6 tablespoons grated parmesan cheese

1 Sauté the onion in the butter
  until soft and transparent.

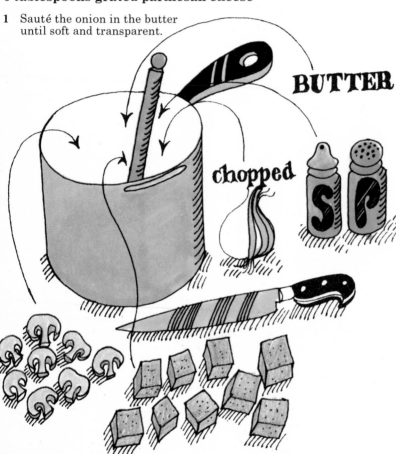

2 Then add the sliced mushrooms and chopped stems,
  turn up the heat slightly, and sauté them until done,
  about 5 minutes. Stir frequently.

3 Add the salt and pepper and the ham squares, and cook
  all together another minute, just to heat through.

4 Add the cream and let everything heat through again, without
  letting the sauce boil. (Be especially careful with fresh
  cream; it may curdle.)
  Then stir in the parsley.

5 Cook the green and yellow noodles separately in plenty of
  boiling water (add salt when boiling) until *al dente*.
  Drain well. (Green noodles cook faster than yellow.)

6 Combine the sauce with the noodles, add the parmesan and
  stir well. Leave them, covered, for 2 minutes before serving.
  You can serve more grated parmesan cheese at the table
  if you wish.

Note You can use all yellow noodles for this dish
  if green noodles are not available.

Paglia e Fieno

A beautifully creamy dish, full of different tastes,
textures and colors. An extremely ingenious blend that is as appealing to the eye
as it is to the tongue, makes a great main course that's easy to make and never fails to please. (Serves 4)

5 tablespoons butter
2 tablespoons flour
1 cup milk
3 oz gouda cheese
3 oz gruyère cheese
3 oz mozzarella cheese
12 oz mostaccioli
4 tablespoons butter
generous grating of black pepper
3 oz grated parmesan cheese

3   Cook the mostaccioli in plenty of boiling water (add salt when boiling) until *al dente*. Drain. Transfer them to a hot dish, flake the remaining 4 tablespoons of butter into the pasta and toss well.

4   Re-heat the cheese sauce if it has cooled too much, and stir to make sure all the cheeses have melted.

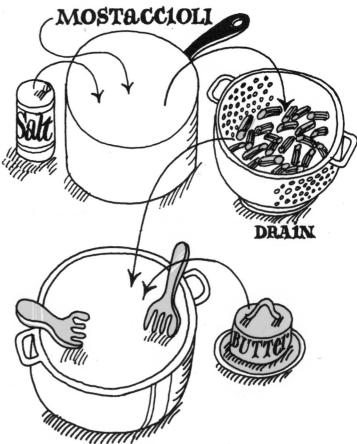

1   To make a white sauce, melt the 5 tablespoons of butter in a saucepan, add the flour all at once, and stir it around until all the flour has been absorbed into the butter. Then add the milk slowly, stirring all the time with a wire whisk, until the sauce starts to thicken. Simmer gently, stirring all the time, for 2 minutes.

5   Pour this sauce over the pasta, sprinkle on the pepper, and toss well to distribute the sauce evenly.

6   Serve immediately, with the grated parmesan passed separately.

2   Grate the first three cheeses on the coarse side of a grater and stir them into the white sauce. It will melt the cheese.

Note   Other cheeses you can add or substitute are provolone, fontina, taleggio or emmenthaler. Instead of parmesan you could use asiago. Macaroni or elbow macaroni can be substituted.

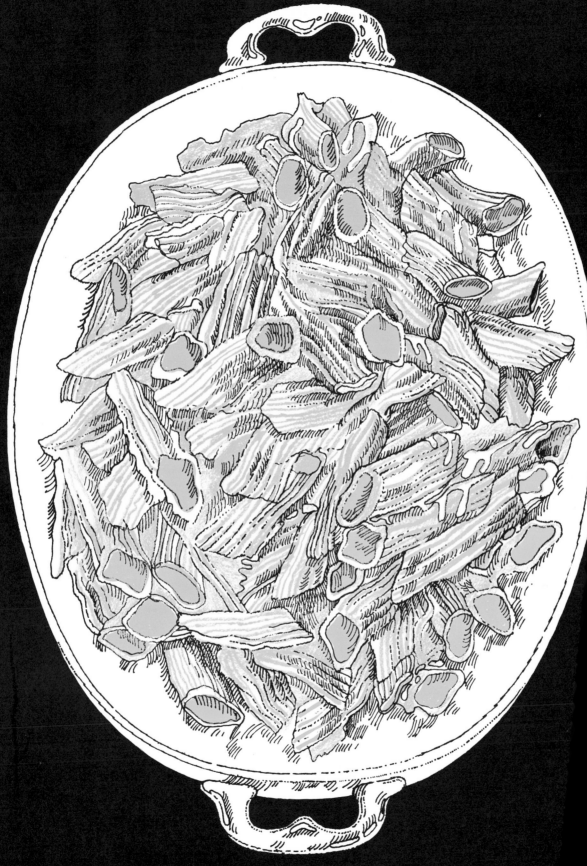

The most cheesy dish you ever tasted.
Full of creamy goodness, with a wonderful bite to it if you use mostaccioli, penne or riga
— the cheese spills over into the holes and you get twice the cheese with every bite. (Serv

18–24 cherrystone clams
7 tablespoons olive oil
3 cloves garlic, cut into quarters
3 tablespoons chopped parsley
$\frac{1}{4}$ teaspoon dried red pepper flakes
$\frac{1}{4}$ teaspoon dried basil
2 shallots *or* 1 small onion, finely chopped
1 cup white wine
1 pound linguine

1   Scrub the clams well with a stiff brush, until all traces
    of sand have disappeared. You may want to soak them
    in cold water for
    a while. Rinse well.

2   Heat the oil in a large saucepan wide enough to accom-
    modate the clams. Put in the garlic quarters and heat
    them through without browning, just for a minute or two.
    Remove the garlic with a slotted spoon.

CHOPPED

SHALLOTS

3   To the oil add the parsley, red pepper flakes,
    basil and shallots or onions and sauté over medium heat,
    stirring frequently, for about 3 minutes.

4   Add the wine and all the clams, cover and leave to simmer
    for 7 minutes. After 7 minutes, tilt the pot back and
    forth a few times to release the clam juices into the wine.
    Uncover.

5   Remove the clams with a slotted spoon onto a plate
    and leave to cool slightly. Remove the clams from
    their shells and cut them into quarters. Put them
    back into the sauce.

CLAMS NOW OPEN

TAKE OUT   & CHOP

6   Cook the linguine in plenty of boiling
    water (add salt when boiling)
    until *al dente*. Drain well.

LINGUINE

7   Transfer the linguine onto a platter
    and spoon the clam sauce on top.

    Serve immediately.

Note   If using canned minced clams follow stages 2 and 3, but at stage 4
       use only half the wine and $\frac{1}{2}$ cup of bottled clam juice.
       Then add the clams and all their juice and cook, uncovered, for
       8–10 minutes to reduce the liquid somewhat. Proceed with stages
       6 and 7. Instead of linguine, you can use spaghetti.

LINGUINE CON VONGOLE

A slightly extravagant seafood dish. The clam juice,
combined with the wine and herbs, produces a beautiful taste and aroma.
A perfect example of the versatility of pasta cookery.
Makes an outstanding first course for six, or a lavish main course for four.

one 2–3 pound chicken
about 5 cups of cold water
1 teaspoon salt
2 tablespoons (1 oz) butter
½ pound fresh mushrooms, sliced
4 tablespoons butter
7 tablespoons flour
2 cups reserved chicken stock
1 cup milk
1 cup heavy cream
salt and pepper to taste
8–12 oz vermicelli
4 tablespoons dry breadcrumbs
4 tablespoons grated parmesan
   cheese

16 fl. oz reserved stock

3   Melt the 4 tablespoons butter in
a heavy saucepan, and when melted
stir in the flour. Mix well with
a wooden spoon or wire whisk, and stir in the reserved stock and the milk.

Cook this mixture over a medium heat until it thickens,
then leave to simmer, stirring all the time, for 3 minutes.
Remove from heat and stir in the cream, salt and pepper.
Add the reserved chicken pieces and the reserved
mushrooms.

VERMICELLI

1   Boil the chicken in salted water until tender, about
40–50 minutes. Remove the chicken, place on a plate
and leave to cool slightly. Reserve 2 cups
of the cooking water to use as stock. When the chicken
is cool enough to handle, skin and bone it carefully
and cut the meat into bite-size pieces.

2   Melt the 2 tablespoons of butter in a frying pan and
sauté the mushrooms until cooked, stirring frequently.
Reserve.

4   Cook the vermicelli in plenty of boiling water
(add salt when boiling) until *al dente*. Drain.

5   Butter a large casserole or ovenproof baking dish. Combine the
sauce and the pasta thoroughly and pour the mixture
into the dish. Smooth the top with the back of a spoon.

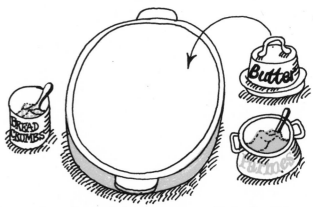

6   Sprinkle the crumbs and grated cheese on top, and bake the dish, uncovered, in a pre-heated (375°) oven for 20–30
minutes. Serve more grated cheese separately if wanted.

Note   This dish can be made up to 2 hours in advance up to stage 5. Keep
covered with foil or plastic until ready to bake. Thin spaghetti
or regular spaghetti can be substituted for vermicelli.

Vermicelli e Pollo

A magnificently smooth, creamy dish. Very attractive
and mouthwatering, so subtle it almost melts on the
tongue, it makes a luxurious lunch or dinner for a reasonable
price. Great as a main course with a tossed salad
and a glass of white wine. Bravo! (Serves 4)

1 recipe egg-noodle dough, cut into cannelloni
   (page 11) *or* 1 package of 12 store-bought cannelloni
1 medium onion, chopped
2 tablespoons oil
1 clove garlic, chopped
1 pound ground beef
one 10-oz package frozen spinach (*or* 1 lb fresh spinach),
   cooked and chopped
2 beaten eggs
5 tablespoons grated parmesan cheese
3 tablespoons cream *or* evaporated milk
salt, pepper and oregano to taste
more parmesan to taste
1 recipe besciamella sauce from page 64
1 recipe tomato sauce from page 64

5   In a mixing bowl combine the beef mixture, spinach, eggs, grated parmesan, cream, salt, pepper and oregano. Mix it all up with a fork until well blended.

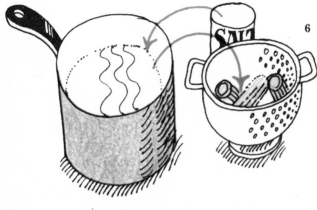

1   Boil the pasta pieces, a few at a time, in plenty of boiling water (add salt when boiling) until *al dente.* Drain and leave to cool slightly.

Oil

chopped onion

chopped garlic

ground beef

2   Sauté the chopped onion in the oil until soft and transparent. Add the garlic and sauté one minute longer.

3   Add the beef, breaking up any lumps with a wooden spoon, until it is brown and crumbly.

4   Cook the spinach, drain well and leave to cool a little.

6   If using homemade squares of dough: place one heaping teaspoon of this filling onto each square of pasta. Fold both sides towards the middle and place each cannelloni, seam side down, into a baking dish which has a thin layer of tomato sauce in it. Don't crowd them, or they will stick together. Store-bought cannelloni tubes can be filled with a teaspoon. Place cannelloni in a single layer all over baking dish. (Scatter leftover filling over them.)

store-bought

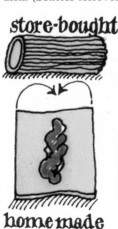

home made

Besciamella

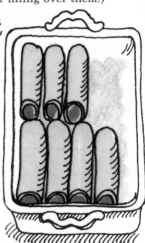

7   Distribute the besciamella evenly over the cannelloni. Then cover the besciamella layer with the rest of the tomato sauce, and sprinkle with parmesan.

Parmesan

8   Bake in a pre-heated oven (375°) for 20 minutes if you ar baking the dish straight away If it has been allowed to get cold, bake it for 40 minutes.

Note

This dish can be made up stage 7 two to three hour advance. Keep covered w foil or plastic until ready to bake.

A truly delectable dish, very popular the world over. The fine combination of meat, spinach and parmesan makes this dish extremely rich in protein. It is very filling and makes a great main course if served with crusty warm bread, a tossed salad and a glass of red wine. Who could ask for anything more? (Serves 4–6)

3 tablespoons butter
1 can tuna fish in oil (6–7 oz)
2 tablespoons finely chopped parsley
1 cup heavy cream
salt and pepper to taste
8 oz margherita

3 Cook the margherita in plenty of boiling water (add salt when boiling) until *al dente*. Drain thoroughly.

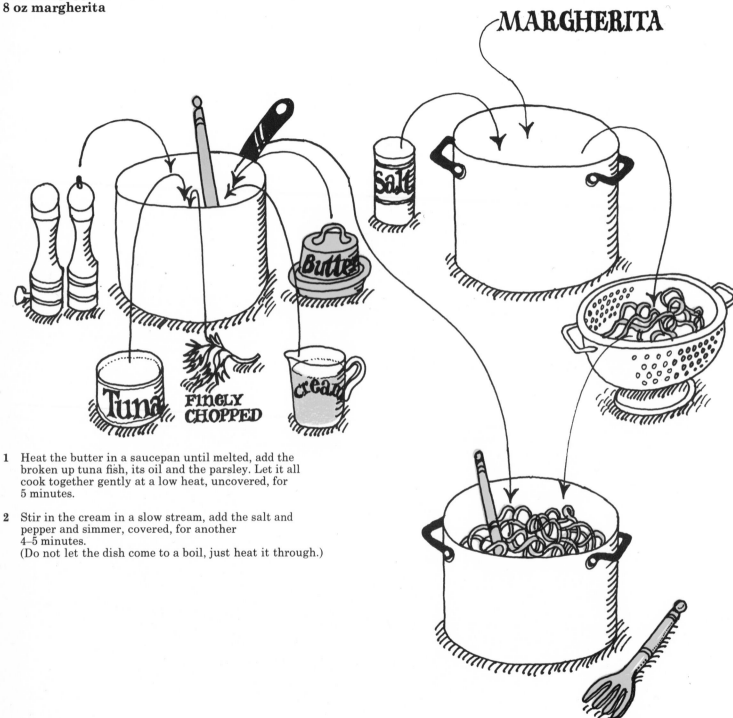

MARGHERITA

1 Heat the butter in a saucepan until melted, add the broken up tuna fish, its oil and the parsley. Let it all cook together gently at a low heat, uncovered, for 5 minutes.

2 Stir in the cream in a slow stream, add the salt and pepper and simmer, covered, for another 4–5 minutes.
(Do not let the dish come to a boil, just heat it through.)

4 Mix the margherita with the tuna sauce, preferably using two wooden forks, until well blended.

Serve immediately.

Note   Tagliatelle or fettuccine can be substituted for margherita.

34

MARGHERITA CON TONNO

A piquant pasta dish, that is at the same time creamy and delicate. Very easy to prepare, fairly inexpensive to make, and a good way to please your friends when you are in a hurry.

And, it's just what children like – tuna fish and noodles. This dish serves two as a delightful lunch, or four as a first course.

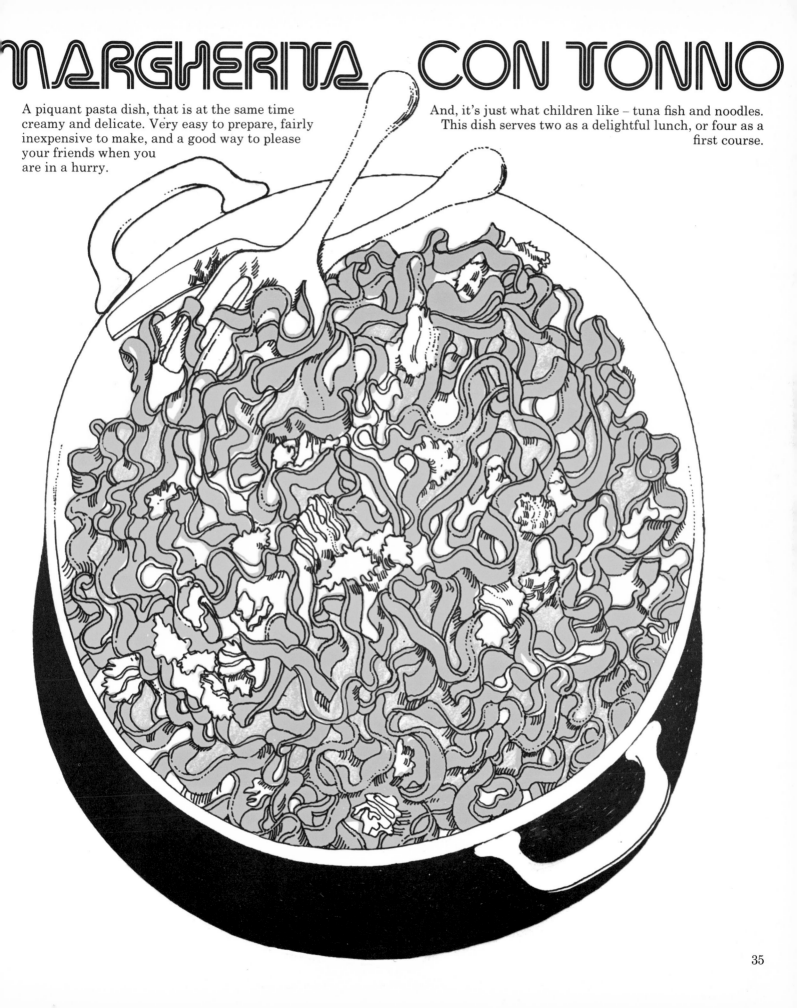

1 onion, finely chopped
3 tablespoons oil
2 cloves garlic, crushed
3 pounds fresh tomatoes,
   skinned and chopped
salt and pepper to taste
1 teaspoon sugar
½ teaspoon dried basil
1 pound raw shrimp, peeled
1 cup white wine
2 tablespoons chopped parsley
1 pound linguine

1 Sauté the onion in the oil until soft and transparent. Add the garlic and sauté one minute longer.

3 Meanwhile, in another saucepan, simmer the peeled shrimp in the wine for 3–4 minutes. Add them to the tomatoes when the tomatoes are cooked. Also add the chopped parsley and let it all simmer another 4–5 minutes.

Finely chopped

CHOPPED

SKIN & CHOP

4 Boil the linguine in plenty of boiling water (add salt when boiling) until *al dente*. Drain.

linguine

Drain

5 Mix the linguine and the shrimp sauce until well combined. Divide the pasta between six small individual dishes, and spoon any sauce that has accumulated in the bottom of the saucepan over the pasta.

Serve immediately.

2 Put the tomatoes in the saucepan with the onions, together with the salt, pepper, sugar and basil. Simmer slowly, uncovered, for 20 minutes.

Note Use only raw shrimp for this dish.
Spaghetti can be substituted for linguine.

Linguine alla Marinara

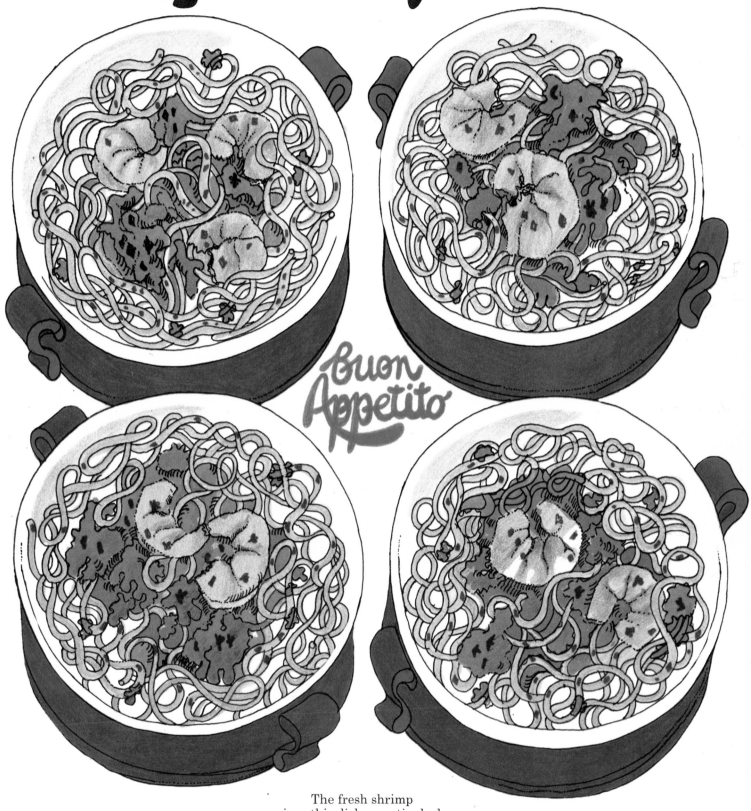

Buon Appetito

The fresh shrimp
gives this dish a particularly
distinguished flavor typical of the Adriatic
coast. The fresh tomatoes add color and gusto. It is the combination
of these light authentic flavors that makes this dish especially pleasant
as a first course in summer. (Serves 6)

1 recipe green-noodle dough from page 8,
    cut into tagliatelle
    or 12 oz green noodles, store-bought
$\frac{1}{4}$–$\frac{3}{8}$ pound soft butter
1–3 cloves garlic, crushed
8 tablespoons grated parmesan cheese
black pepper and salt to taste

1   Cook the tagliatelle in plenty of water (add salt
    when boiling) until *al dente*. Drain.

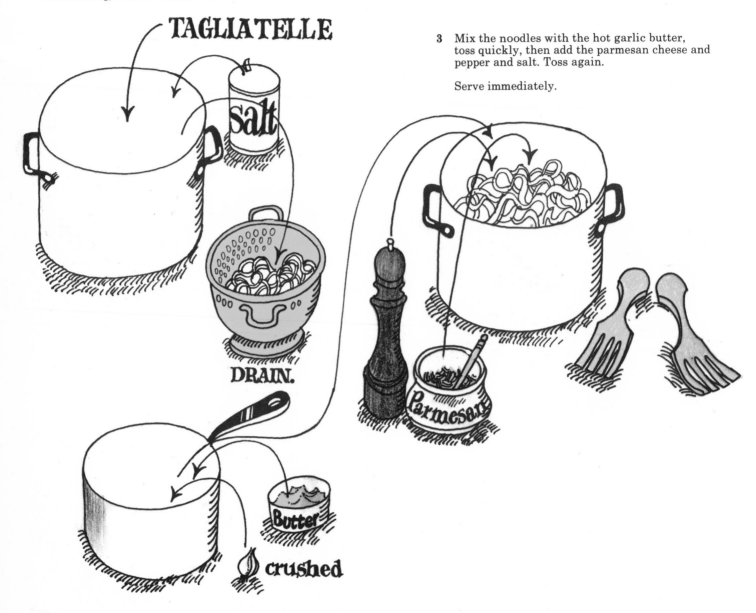

TAGLIATELLE

salt

DRAIN.

Butter

crushed

3   Mix the noodles with the hot garlic butter,
    toss quickly, then add the parmesan cheese and
    pepper and salt. Toss again.

    Serve immediately.

Parmesan

2   While the pasta is cooking, heat the butter in another
    saucepan and sauté the garlic in it over a very low heat.
    Do not let either the butter or the garlic brown.
    Sauté only for a minute.

Note   This recipe is especially good
       with homemade green noodles.

TAGLIATELLE VERDI CON AGLIO

Buon Appetito

One of those melt-in-the-mouth pasta dishes, incredibly smooth and creamy, with a glorious color and a mild or strong garlic flavor, whichever you prefer. A marvelous first course for four or five, or a great side dish with fried, roast or grilled meat.

1½ **pounds ricotta cheese**
2 **beaten eggs**
3 **tablespoons finely chopped parsley**
a little grated nutmeg
2 **tablespoons grated parmesan** *or* **romano cheese**
2 **oz grated** *or* **finely chopped mozzarella cheese**
1 **recipe egg-noodle dough from page 8,**
  cut into manicotti,
  or **1 package of 12 store-bought manicotti**
double the recipe for tomato sauce on page 64
5 **tablespoons grated parmesan**

3   Cook the manicotti in plenty of boiling water (add salt when boiling) until *al dente*. (Cook a few at a time.) Drain and leave to cool slightly.

drain

1   Drain the ricotta cheese well.

4   If using homemade pasta squares, place a heaping tablespoon of cheese filling on each rectangle, then fold both sides towards the middle to cover the filling. (Store-bought manicotti tubes can be filled with a teaspoon.)

store~bought

homemade
square

5   Spread a thin layer of the tomato sauce in a buttered, ovenproof baking dish. Lay the manicotti, seam side down and not touching, in a single layer in the dish. Pour the rest of the tomato sauce over the top.

2   Place the ricotta in a mixing bowl, add the eggs, parsley, nutmeg and the grated cheeses. Blend well with a fork.

eggs~beaten

parsley~
finely chopped

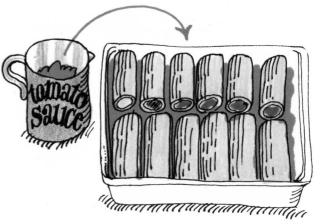

6   Sprinkle the parmesan cheese on top and bake, uncovered, in a pre-heated (325°) oven for about 30 minutes.

Note   This dish can be made up to 2 hours in advance up to stage 5. Keep the dish covered with foil or plastic until ready to put it in the oven.

40

Manicotti

In outward appearance manicotti somewhat resemble
cannelloni. However, this manicotti recipe oozes its own taste of a
savory cheese filling topped with a delicious tomato sauce.
Extremely satisfying, very Italian and very appetizing. (Serves 4–6)

2 tablespoons oil
1 large onion, finely chopped
1–2 cloves garlic, crushed (optional)
1 green pepper, cut into strips
black pepper to taste
dried tarragon to taste
1 recipe tomato sauce from page 64
1 pound cod *or* **sole** *or* **haddock, cubed**
1 pound tagliatelle

1 Heat the oil in a heavy saucepan, then add the chopped onion, crushed garlic, green pepper strips and sauté it all until soft, about 8 minutes. Then add the black pepper and tarragon.

3 Cook the tagliatelle in plenty of boiling water (add salt when boiling) until *al dente*. Drain.

TAGLIATELLE

tomato sauce

FISH

4 Mix the noodles into the tomato-fish sauce, combining them well.

2 To the saucepan add the tomato sauce and the chunks of fish. Cook the dish, uncovered, for about 10 minutes, until the fish is tender but not falling apart.

Tagliatelle e Pesce

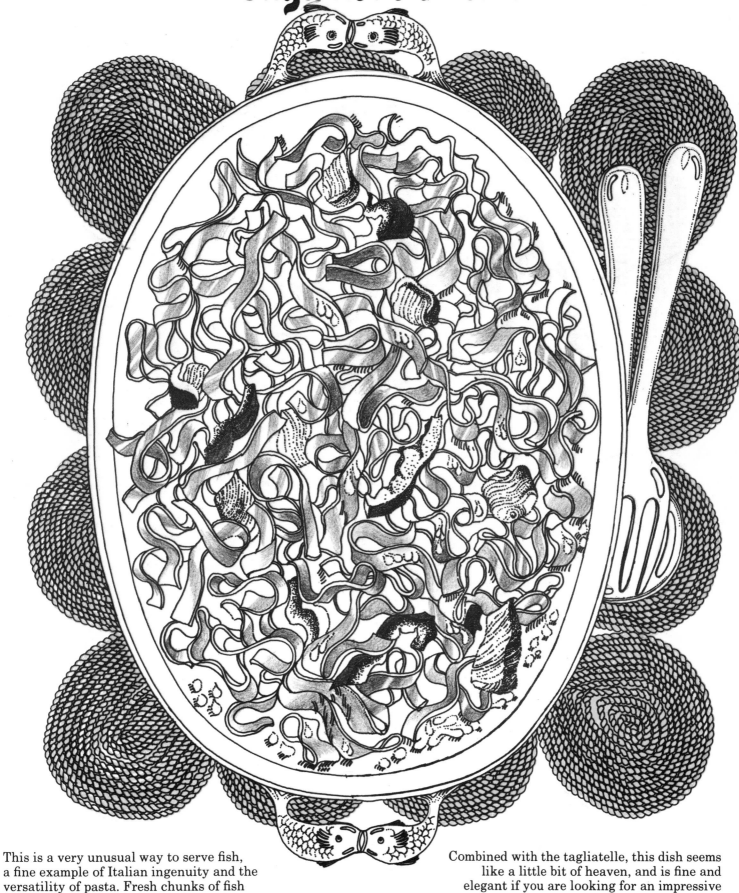

This is a very unusual way to serve fish, a fine example of Italian ingenuity and the versatility of pasta. Fresh chunks of fish bathed in a delicate, delicious tomato sauce.

Combined with the tagliatelle, this dish seems like a little bit of heaven, and is fine and elegant if you are looking for an impressive and unusual fish course for six. Buon appetito!

3 tablespoons butter
1 pound fresh mushrooms,
   whole if small, sliced if large
2 tablespoons oil
1 pound ground pork
1–2 cloves garlic, crushed
½ teaspoon dried basil
½ teaspoon dried oregano

salt and pepper to taste
½ cup white wine
2 tablespoons flour
3 tablespoons tomato paste
1 cup beef stock
12 oz farfalloni
freshly grated parmesan
   cheese

4 Add the tomato paste and the stock. Stir well,
   cover, and leave to simmer over a low flame for
   about 20 minutes. Stir quite often to prevent
   it burning. When done, add the reserved mushrooms.

FARFALLONI

1 In a saucepan melt the butter and over medium heat sauté
   the mushrooms until cooked, stirring often. Set aside.

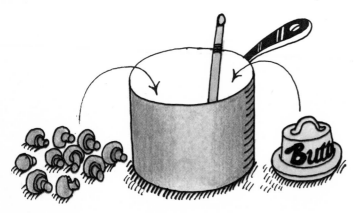

5 Cook the farfalloni in plenty of boiling water
   (add salt when boiling) until *al dente*. Drain.

6 Mix together the farfalloni and the meat-mushroom
   sauce and serve immediately. Pass the grated
   parmesan separately.

2 In another saucepan heat the oil and brown the pork in it,
   breaking up any lumps with a wooden spoon. (At this point
   I like to pour off all the fat, see page 11.)
   Stir into the meat the garlic, basil, oregano, salt and pepper. Leave to cook for
   2 minutes.

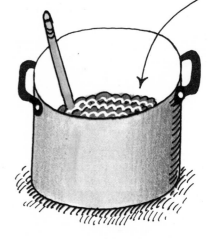

Note This sauce can be made hours in advance; just
          reheat it while the pasta is cooking.
          This dish is also good when made with egg
          noodles of any width.

3 Turn up the heat and pour in the wine. Let it boil rapidly
   until the foam subsides. Then add in all the flour, stirring well.

Farfalloni con Funghi

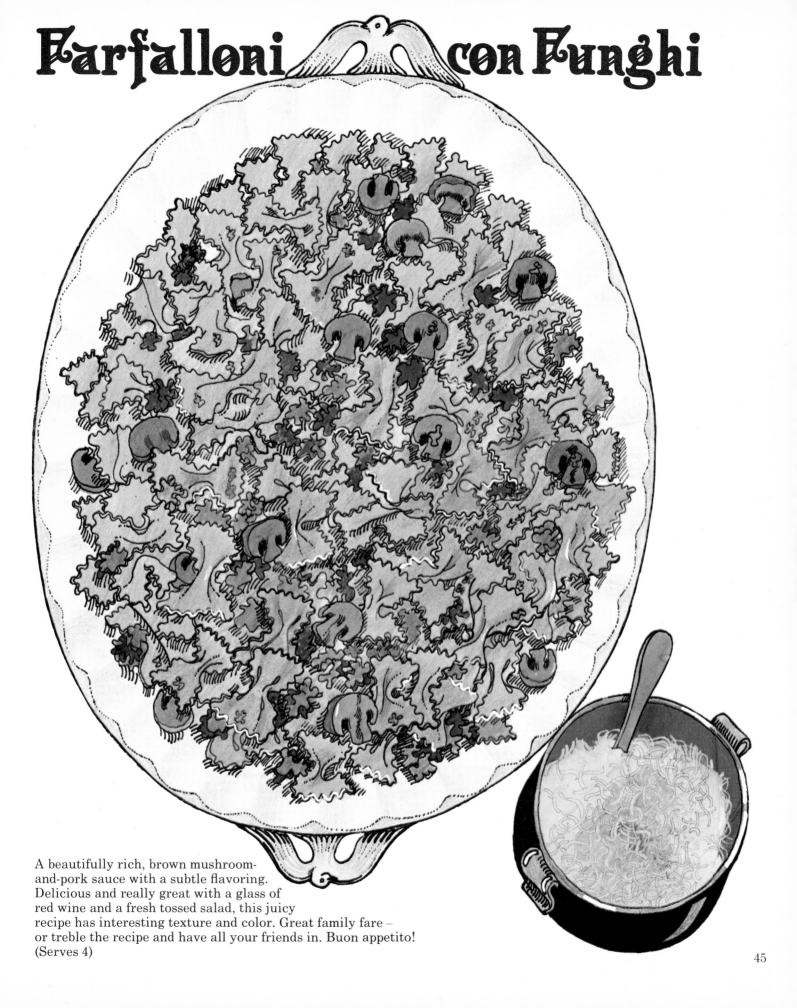

A beautifully rich, brown mushroom-
and-pork sauce with a subtle flavoring.
Delicious and really great with a glass of
red wine and a fresh tossed salad, this juicy
recipe has interesting texture and color. Great family fare –
or treble the recipe and have all your friends in. Buon appetito!
(Serves 4)

12 oz fettuccine
½ cup heavy cream
4–8 tablespoons softened butter
8 tablespoons grated parmesan cheese
6 oz fresh or frozen peas, cooked
½ pound thinly sliced prosciutto *or* boiled ham,
   cut into thin strips
black pepper to taste

3 Drain the fettuccine, pour them back into the
    pot and quickly toss in the flaked soft butter
    and the parmesan.

1 Cook the fettuccine in plenty of boiling water
    (add salt when boiling) until *al dente*.

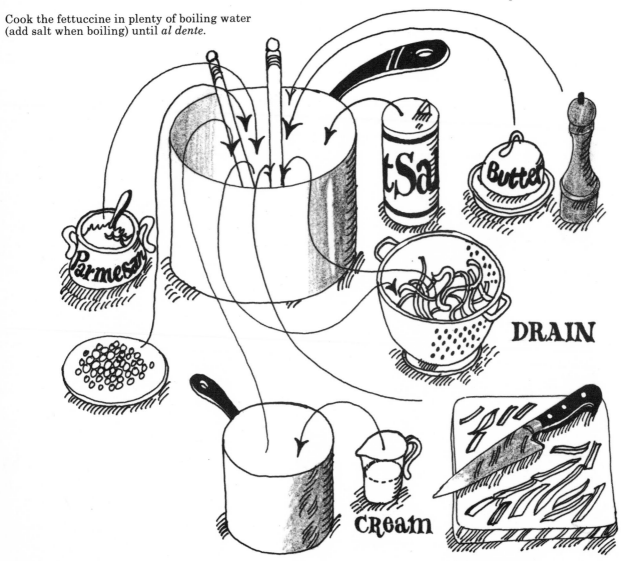

2 While the pasta is cooking, heat the cream
    in a small saucepan.

4 Add the hot cream, the peas, the prosciutto
    and black pepper and toss again.

    Serve immediately.

Fettuccine alla Romana

A deliciously creamy, colorful dish, the way it is served in Rome.
One of our many favorites, just too good for words, super for a quick lunch.
Invite your friends, bring out the wine and the good conversation.
Buon appetito. (Serves 4)

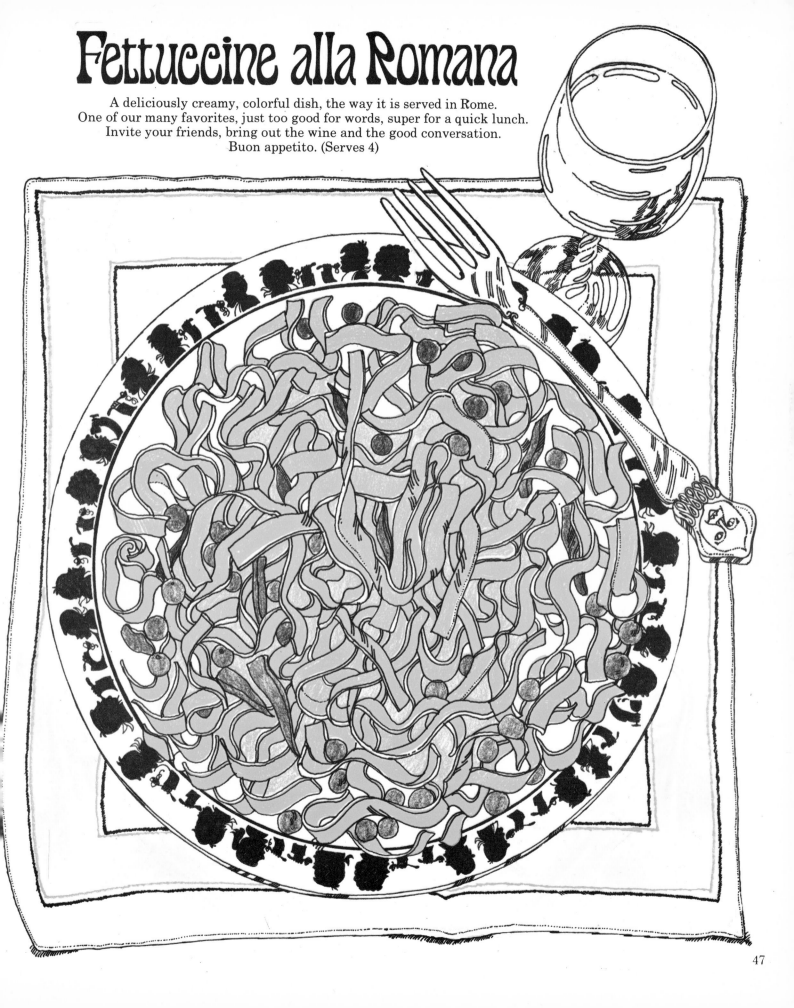

2 tablespoons oil
1 onion, finely chopped
1 red pepper (green if red is unavailable), cut into strips
1 clove garlic, chopped
1 tablespoon chopped parsley
½ pound lean bacon, cut into strips
1 pound fresh tomatoes, peeled and roughly chopped
  or **1 (16 oz) can tomatoes**
generous grating of black pepper
12 oz spaghetti
2 tablespoons oil
4 tablespoons grated parmesan *or* **romano cheese**

1   Heat the oil in a saucepan and add the onion, red or green
    pepper, garlic, parsley and bacon. Sauté for about 5 minutes,
    uncovered and stirring often.

2   To this mixture add the tomatoes and pepper. Simmer this dish,
    uncovered, for 15 minutes. Add a little salt then if necessary.

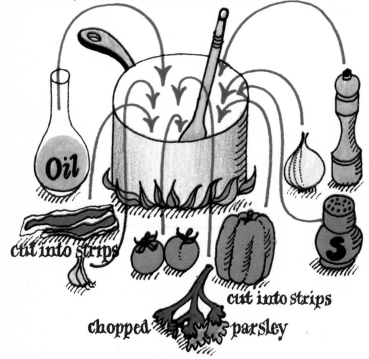

cut into strips
chopped   parsley
cut into strips

4   Place the spaghetti in a hot bowl,
    sprinkle on the oil and cheese and toss well.

3   Cook the spaghetti in plenty of boiling water
    (add salt when boiling) until *al dente*. Drain.

5   Serve the pasta in individual small bowls,
    with the sauce spooned on top.

    Serve immediately.

Note   The sauce itself can be made several hours
           in advance and reheated.

Spaghetti all'Amatriciana

Spaghetti All'Amatriciana takes its name from Amatrice,
a small town north of Rome, famous because generations
of grocers came from there. Fullbodied and robust taste,
a juicy blend of pasta, vegetables, meat and cheese.
A great light lunch for three or four, or a first course
for five or six.

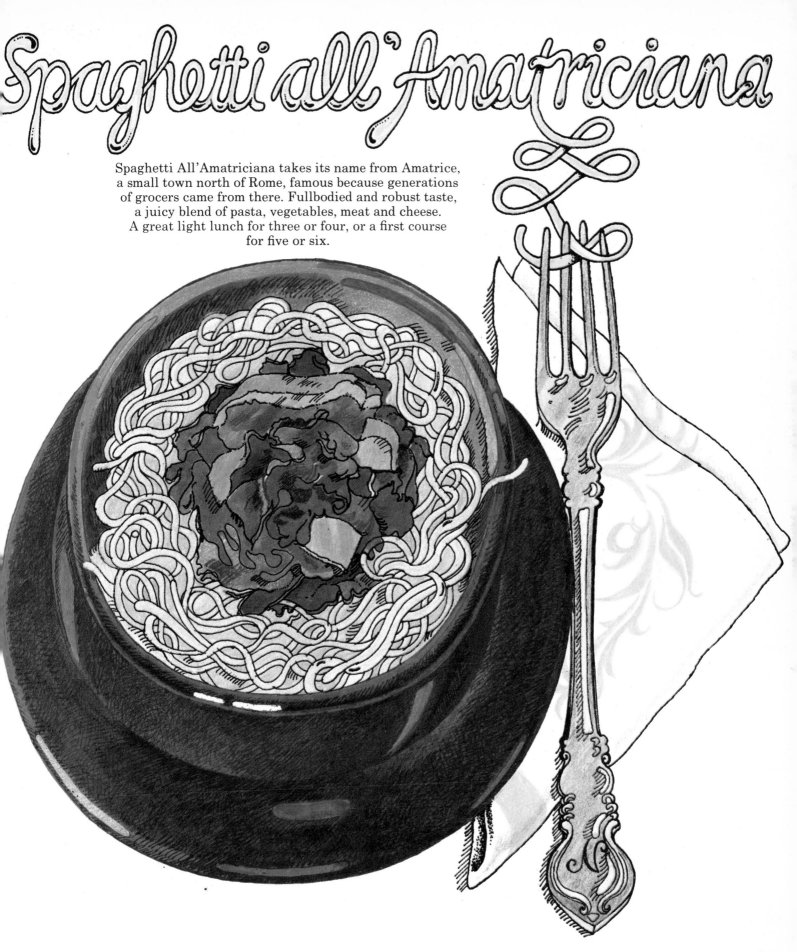

1 medium sized eggplant
salt
6 medium sized tomatoes, peeled,
   seeded and chopped
1–2 cloves garlic, crushed
1–2 tablespoons parsley, chopped
½ teaspoon dried red pepper flakes
2 tablespoons butter
enough oil for frying eggplant
1 pound spaghetti

3 In a frying pan sauté the eggplant slices in some hot oil. They will absorb the oil quite quickly, so keep adding more as needed. Fry the slices till they are golden brown on both sides.

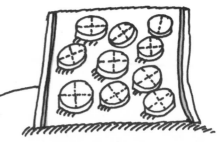

4 Drain the slices on paper towels to absorb the excess fat, then cut them into halves or quarters, and add them to the tomato sauce. Heat through again while the pasta is cooking. Taste for seasoning.

5 Cook the spaghetti in plenty of boiling water (add salt when boiling) until *al dente*. Drain.

1 Cut off both ends of the eggplant and cut the remaining piece into ¼-inch-thick slices. Put the slices into a non-metal bowl, sprinkle a little salt on them, and leave them to drain for 30–45 minutes. After that, dry them thoroughly with paper towels.

SPAGHETTI

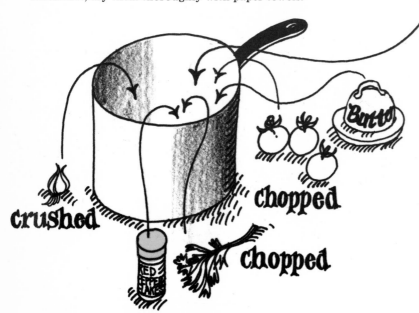

crushed

chopped

chopped

6 Serve the pasta on individual hot plates, with the sauce spooned on top.

2 Meanwhile sauté the chopped tomatoes, garlic, parsley and red pepper flakes in the butter in a saucepan for about 5 minutes. Reserve.

50

A delightful light summer lunch, colorful and unusual.
You can taste the summer goodness of fresh vegetables,
a truly Sicilian combination of tastes.
The more you eat it, the more you'll like it.
(Serves 4)

1 recipe egg-noodle dough from page 8
1 pound ricotta cheese
2 oz parmesan cheese, grated
3 tablespoons chopped parsley
a little salt and pepper
1 medium egg

a little grated nutmeg
1 recipe either tomato sauce, bolognese sauce *or*
    beef sauce from page 64, *or* just melted butter and
    parmesan cheese
grated parmesan cheese

1 Prepare the filling by combining in a bowl the ricotta, parmesan, parsley, salt, pepper, egg and nutmeg. Blend it all well with a fork.

Parmesan   nutmeg

2 Roll out the dough to ⅛-inch thickness. Cut the dough into 2-inch circles, with a biscuit-cutter or glass of that diameter.

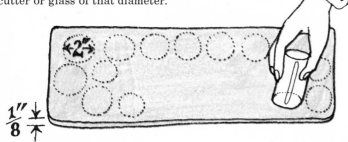

3 Place about ½ teaspoon of filling on each circle.

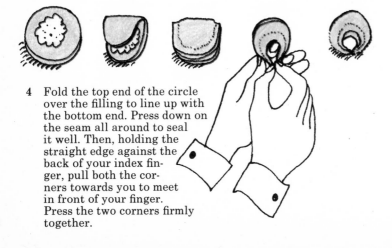

4 Fold the top end of the circle over the filling to line up with the bottom end. Press down on the seam all around to seal it well. Then, holding the straight edge against the back of your index finger, pull both the corners towards you to meet in front of your finger. Press the two corners firmly together.

5 Place the finished tortellini in a single layer (not allowing them to touch) on a well-floured waxed paper or greaseproof paper and proceed to shape the rest.

6 Boil the tortellini, a few at a time, in plenty of boiling water (add salt when boiling) until *al dente*. Drain well.

Drain

7 Serve hot, with one of the sauces spooned on top. Serve plenty of grated parmesan cheese separately.

Note You can make tortellini a few hours ahead. Keep them on a well-floured, paper-lined tray, not touching one another, and dust them heavily with flour. Keep refrigerated until ready to use.

Tortellini

One of the glorious stuffed-pasta dishes. When served without a meat-sauce they are called Tortellini da Vigilia (lean tortellini). They are served thus on religious holidays, when the eating of meat is not permitted. (Serves six as a first course, four as a main course.)

1 pound lean lamb, cubed
salt and pepper to taste
¼ teaspoon dried rosemary
3 tablespoons oil
1–2 cloves garlic, chopped
⅜ cup white wine
1 pound fresh tomatoes,
    peeled and chopped
¾–1 cup beef stock
8 oz cavatelli
grated parmesan cheese

1 Season the lamb cubes with a little salt, pepper and rosemary.

5 Cook the cavatelli in plenty of boiling water (add salt when boiling) until *al dente*. Drain.

2 Heat the oil in a saucepan over fairly high heat and brown the meat cubes on all sides. Add the garlic and cook 1 minute longer.

3 Pour the wine over the meat and let it boil, uncovered, until the foam subsides.

4 Stir in the tomatoes and stock and simmer, only partially covered, for 1–1½ hours. Stir frequently. The sauce will reduce to about half and be fairly thick. Adjust seasoning.

6 Combine the pasta and the sauce, then stir in the parmesan cheese.

Serve immediately, with plenty of freshly grated parmesan passed separately.

Note Instead of cavatelli you can use macaroni, rotini, mostaccioli, rigatoni, conchiglie or farfalloni.

54

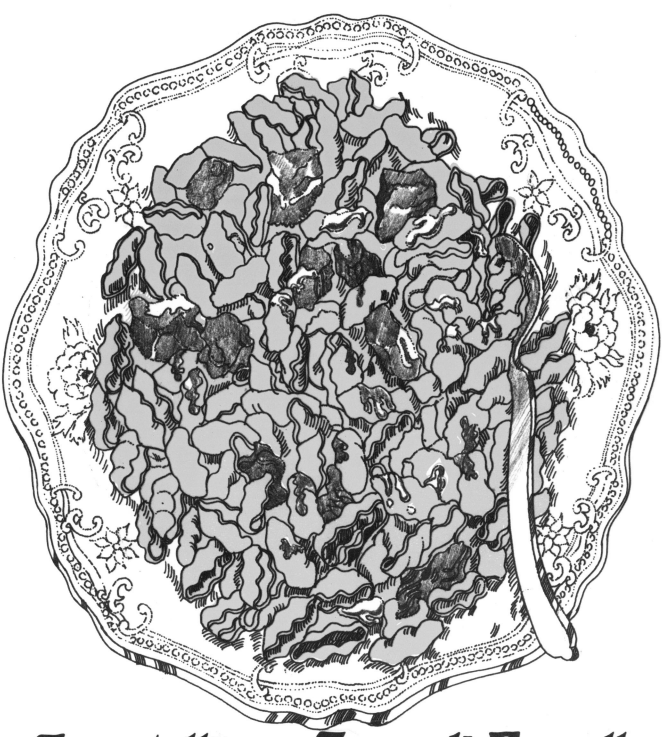

Cavatelli con Sugo di Agnello

Country character is what makes this dish so hearty and delightful.
The succulent pieces of lamb combine extremely well with the rich tomato sauce,
which in turn complements this unusual pasta shape. Great family fare.
(Serves 3–4)

2 tablespoons oil
1 large onion, finely chopped
1 clove garlic, crushed
3 slices bacon, chopped
one 1-pound can tomatoes
   or 1 pound fresh tomatoes,
   peeled and chopped

salt and pepper to taste
½ teaspoon dried basil
1 tablespoon butter
½ pound chicken livers, chopped
1 pound fettucce
1 more tablespoon butter

1   Heat the oil in a heavy saucepan and sauté the onion, garlic and bacon over medium heat for 5 minutes.

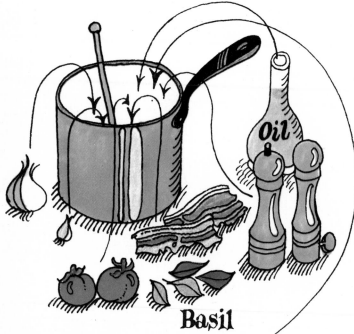

2   To this mixture add the tomatoes, salt, pepper and basil. Break up the tomatoes with a wooden spoon. Simmer the sauce, uncovered, for about 20 minutes.

3   Melt the butter in a frying pan and sauté the chicken livers for 3–4 minutes.

4   Mix the livers with the tomato sauce and simmer it all together, covered, for 2 minutes, just to heat it through.

5   Cook the fettucce in plenty of boiling water (add salt when boiling) until *al dente*. Drain. Return to saucepan and toss in the remaining butter.

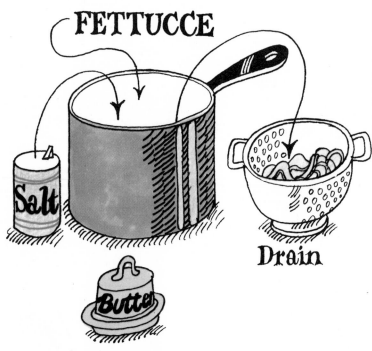

6   Divide the pasta between 5–6 individual bowls, and spoon a generous amount of sauce on top of each one.

Serve immediately.

Note   The sauce can be prepared a few hours ahead and reheated while the pasta is cooking. Fettuccine, tagliatelle or pappardelle can be substituted for fettucce.

Fettucce con Fegatini di Pollo

A savory sauce that goes extremely well with wide egg noodles.
Exquisitely flavored, with a hearty bite to it.
A great light lunch for four,
or an unusual first course for six.
Bravissimo!

2 fennels
1 large onion, chopped
2 tablespoons olive oil
2 anchovy fillets, chopped
1 heaping tablespoon raisins,
　soaked in water for 1 hour
1 tablespoon almonds *or* **pine nuts**
a pinch of saffron
salt and pepper to taste
8 oz fresh sardines
1 pound conchiglie

1　Boil the fennels in plenty of salted water until
　al dente. (Test as you would potatoes.) Drain them well,
　and reserve the cooking water.

4　Slice the somewhat cooled fennels into ½-inch
　thick slices and add them to the pot.

5　Cook the shells in the reserved cooking water
　until *al dente.* Drain well. (If the reserved
　cooking water is not enough, make up the
　difference with hot water.)

CONCHIGLIE

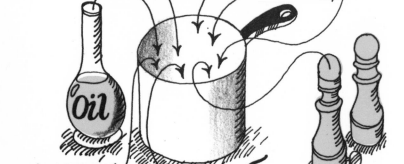

6　Mix the shells and the fennel-sardine
　mixture well and serve immediately.

Note　Since you will probably not be able to buy
　fresh sardines, a small tin of skinned
　and boned sardines may be added at stage 4.

2　Sauté the onion in the olive oil until soft and transparent.

3　Add the anchovy fillets, the raisins, the almonds,
　saffron, salt, pepper and the sardines. Cook over low heat,
　stirring gently from time to time, for 8 minutes.

Conchiglie alla Siciliana

A real Sicilian pasta dish that includes exotic foods grown under the Sicilian sun, such as typically Italian fennel and anchovies. A mildly zesty taste that echoes the flavor of foreign parts, this is a real treat for the gourmets or pasta addicts who think they have eaten everything.
Serves four as a main course,
six as a first course.

3 tablespoons oil
2 cloves garlic, crushed
1 small tin anchovies, chopped
2 tablespoons chopped parsley
one 1-pound can tomatoes
salt and pepper to taste
1 pound spaghetti

3   Stir in the tomatoes, salt and pepper and bring the mixture to a gentle boil. Let it simmer, uncovered, for 30 minutes, stirring now and then.

1   Heat the oil in a small saucepan and sauté the garlic for 1 minute without browning it.

2   Add the chopped anchovy fillets and the parsley and cook it all for a few seconds, just to heat it through.

4   Cook the spaghetti in plenty of boiling water (add salt when boiling) until *al dente*. Drain.

5   Mix the spaghetti and the sauce to coat the pasta evenly.

Serve immediately.

Note   You can make the sauce well in advance if you wish.

SPAGHETTI AL SUGO DI POMODORO E ACCIUGHE

The true taste of Italian cuisine, colorful and full of flavor.
A unique combination of ingredients, blending so well that even non-Italians will love this dish.
Very inexpensive and easy. Great as a first course for six.

1 pound hot Italian sausage, skin removed
2 tablespoons oil
1 green pepper, chopped
1 medium onion, chopped
2 tablespoons butter
one 2-pound can tomatoes
salt and pepper to taste
½ teaspoon dried oregano
1 pound zite
8 oz sliced or shredded mozzarella
6 tablespoons grated parmesan cheese

4   Cook the zite in plenty of boiling water
    (add salt when boiling) until *al dente*. Drain.

1   Brown the sausage meat in the oil, breaking up any
    lumps with a wooden spoon. (Pour off the accumulated
    fat if you wish, see page 11.)

5   Butter an ovenproof baking dish. In it put
    layer of zite, a layer of sauce, a layer of
    mozzarella; repeat, finishing with mozzarel
    Sprinkle some of the parmesan on top.

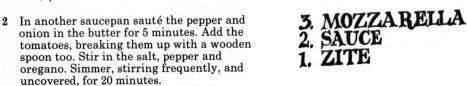

3. MOZZARELLA
2. SAUCE
1. ZITE

2   In another saucepan sauté the pepper and
    onion in the butter for 5 minutes. Add the
    tomatoes, breaking them up with a wooden
    spoon too. Stir in the salt, pepper and
    oregano. Simmer, stirring frequently, and
    uncovered, for 20 minutes.

3   Add the browned sausage meat to the sauce.

6   Bake, uncovered, in a pre-heated (375°)
    oven, for 30 minutes.

    Serve the leftover parmesan separately.

Note   The sauce can of course be made hours ahead
           and reheated while the pasta is cooking.

62

ZITE CON SALSICCIA

A very spicy,
juicy dish to warm
your heart and your stomach.
A cool, tossed salad and a chilled wine are
absolutely essential with this dish. So good, you might
also want a piece of fresh bread to mop up the sauce. (Serves 4)

Sauces

Salsa di Pomodoro
(Basic Tomato Sauce)

1 large onion, chopped
2 tablespoons oil
1 clove garlic, chopped (optional)
1 large 2-pound can tomatoes
or **2 pounds fresh tomatoes, peeled and chopped**
3 level tablespoons tomato paste
1 teaspoon dried basil
½ teaspoon sugar
salt and pepper to taste

Sauté onion in oil until soft and transparent. Do not let the onion brown. Add the garlic (if used) and sauté one minute. Stir in the tomatoes and juice, breaking them up with a wooden spoon. Add the tomato paste, basil, sugar and a pinch of salt and pepper. Simmer the sauce, partially covered, for 30–40 minutes, until it has reduced to a thick consistency that will coat the back of a spoon. Stir sauce often to prevent burning. Strain it through a fine sieve, pressing down hard on the tomatoes and onions. Add more salt and pepper if needed. This makes about 1 pint of sauce which can be used over any kind of pasta or in baked dishes. It will keep for weeks, tightly covered, in the refrigerator, so you can make many times the quantity and use some when needed.

Ragù di Manzo
(Beef Sauce)

1 large onion, finely chopped
2 tablespoons oil
1–3 cloves garlic, crushed (optional)
1 pound ground beef
one 1-pound can tomatoes
or **1 pound fresh tomatoes, peeled and chopped**
2 tablespoons tomato paste
1 teaspoon dried oregano
1 teaspoon dried basil
1 bay leaf
salt and pepper to taste
⅜–½ cup red wine

Sauté onion in oil until soft and transparent. Add garlic and cook another minute. Add ground beef and cook it until brown and crumbly. Break up any lumps with a wooden spoon. Pour off accumulated fat. Stir in tomatoes, breaking them up with a wooden spoon, tomato paste, oregano, basil, bay leaf, and a little salt and pepper. Simmer the sauce, partially covered, stirring often, for 30–40 minutes. Before serving, stir in the wine off the heat. Serve this sauce over any pasta, and serve plenty of grated parmesan with it.

Marinara Sauce

3 tablespoons oil
1 large onion, chopped
1 small carrot, chopped
1–2 cloves garlic, crushed
one 2-pound can tomatoes
or **2 pounds fresh tomatoes, peeled and chopped**
1 teaspoon dried oregano
½ teaspoon dried basil
salt and pepper to taste

Sauté in oil the onion, carrot and garlic for about 5 minutes. Add the tomatoes, breaking them up with a wooden spoon. Add the oregano and basil and simmer, partially covered, for about 30 minutes. Strain sauce through a fine sieve, pushing down hard on the vegetables. Reheat if necessary. If the sauce is too thin, boil it down, uncovered, over a medium heat, until it has reduced to the desired consistency. Season with salt and pepper to taste. This sauce can be served over any kind of pasta.

Ragù Bolognese
(Bolognese Sauce)

3 tablespoons butter
4 slices bacon, chopped
1 large onion, finely chopped
1 medium carrot, finely chopped
1 stalk celery, finely chopped
2 tablespoons oil
⅓ pound ground beef
⅓ pound ground pork
⅓ pound ground veal
½ cup white wine
2 cups beef stock
3 tablespoons tomato paste
1 teaspoon dried oregano
a little grated nutmeg
salt and pepper to taste
1 cup heavy cream (optional)

Melt butter in a frying pan and in it sauté the bacon, onion, carrot and celery. Cook, uncovered, stirring often, for about 10 minutes. Set aside till needed. Heat the oil in another saucepan and in it brown the meats, breaking up any lumps with a wooden spoon, until the mixture is brown and crumbly. Pour off fat, see page 11. Stir in wine over medium high heat letting most of it evaporate. Stir in beef stock, tomato paste, oregano, nutmeg and a little salt and pepper. Add reserved vegetables and bacon. Simmer mixture, partially covered, until it has reduced to a thick sauce, about 40–60 minutes. Add all or some of the cream, if wanted. Don't let it boil again. When served over pasta adding cream rounds off the flavors. But it should not be used in baked dishes incorporating besciamella, such as lasagne, because the dish will lack contrast in color and flavor.

Besciamella
(Bechamel Sauce)

6 tablespoons butter
4 tablespoons flour
2¼ cups milk
salt and pepper to taste
a little ground nutmeg

Melt the butter in a saucepan. Make a roux by adding the flour, and stirring with a wire whisk until the flour has been absorbed by the butter. Don't let it brown! Slowly add the milk, stirring quickly and constantly with a wire whisk. Raise the heat, stirring all the time, until the sauce comes to the boil and thickens. Cook, uncovered, still stirring, for 3 minutes. Season with salt, pepper and nutmeg. This sauce is used in many baked pasta dishes.

Pesto alla Genovese
(Genoese Pesto)

1–3 cloves garlic
¾ pint fresh basil leaves (leaves only)
2–3 oz grated parmesan *or* romano cheese
2 tablespoons finely chopped pine nuts
or **blanched almonds (optional)**
salt and pepper to taste
1¼ cups olive oil

Mash garlic and basil to a smooth paste with a mortar and pestle, or use a bowl and the back of a spoon. Add cheese and nuts, and press them down. Mix in the salt and pepper. Whisk in the oil slowly, in an even stream. The sauce should be very smooth. This sauce can also be made in an electric blender. Blend all ingredients except cheese, at high speed until sauce is smooth and fairly thick. (Push down several times if necessary.) Pour into a bowl. If sauce is too thick, thin down with some oil as required. Blend in the cheese. This sauce can be served over any pasta dish.